I0160121

Ma's Cookbook

Her Language of Love is Food

Jack Warkenthien and Luann Stec

NSS
PUBLISHING

DEDICATION

This demonstration of our love is, of course, dedicated to our mom: Pauline Warkenthien. She is the "reason for the season" and our inspiration for every step we took in creating this book. If you believe the best teachers are the ones whose lives are the texts, Ma is a superb teacher. She walks her talk, says what she means, and means what she says. We always know where we stand when Ma speaks because she speaks her mind. How refreshing, really, and we love her for it.

Of course, Ma wouldn't be here without Ma Ma—and that is our late beloved grandma and Mom's mom—Anna Battaglia. Though we weren't blessed with knowing our grandpa, Frank Battaglia (I'm told I favor him), who passed quite suddenly at the far too early age of fifty-two, we grew up with Grandma. We also dedicate this book to her and have included some of her original recipes from the old, dusty, leather-bound, hand-written book we were given.

I still recall our Sunday afternoon family dinners on Longcommon Road in Riverside, which was a relatively long drive from where we lived in Naperville. The rest of the family lived much closer in. We'd spend hours at the long dining room table as Grandma would bring in dish after dish of the best Italian cooking anywhere. You see, the apple doesn't fall far from the . . . well, you know! Grandma would then sit down after dinner, and the sisters (including Ma) would clean up. Grandma was the quiet matriarch of the family, and everyone loved her. How blessed we were to know her. Enjoy your peek into our dining room on any Sunday afternoon as you sample some of the finest cuisine, compliments of Anna Battaglia and Pauline Warkenthien. I can smell the breaded veal cutlets from here!

© 2010 Jack Warkenthien and Luann Stec

All rights reserved. No part of this book may be used or reproduced in any manner without written permission except in the case of brief quotations embodied in critical articles or reviews.

Ma's Cookbook: Her Language of Love is Food

NextStep Solutions Press
5090 Richmond Ave, Suite 400
Houston, Texas 77056
www.nextstep-solutions.com
210.602.1952

ISBN 978-0-9752737-0-8

Printing in the United States.

For more information please contact,
mascookbook1@gmail.com.

TABLE OF CONTENTS

INTRODUCTION

by Jack Warkenthien

The *Ma's Cookbook* project was actually conceived over five years ago when I first decided it would be nice to memorialize my mother's incredible Italian recipes. Of course, like most other projects in my life, I visualized a profit motive (call me Alex P. Keaton) along the way. Inspired by a San Antonio friend of mine, "Speedy" Gonzalez, who published his mom's Mexican recipes on the internet and made lots of dough (not the kind you knead for bread), I decided to do something similar for Ma. After all, she's the BEST Italian cook on the planet.

As usual, there was a huge gap between my vision and execution (Q: What do you call a vision without a plan? A: A hallucination!). Busyness got in the way, and real life took some unexpected twists and turns, including a significant emotional event or three—just enough distractions for me to delay the project. I'm grateful to Milli Brown, owner and founder of Brown Books, for calling me up and asking where she should return all the recipes I'd given her years ago to do the cookbook. My desire was to create a living, breathing legacy for my Ma and the entire family.

That was the push I needed to kick-start the dream again. I'm not getting any younger, and Ma isn't either. Finally, all the stars lined up in the sky, and I knew it was time to begin. Thank goodness for my favorite sis, Luann, who just so happened to have a couple months of "free time" to do the coordination of all the moving pieces—and there were plenty. We told Ma that she was working on my next book to keep her off the trail.

Pauline Warkenthien is a legend, and every legend deserves to leave a legacy. Her gift of love, appreciation of food, and her ability to bring the family together around it will transcend all of our lives and thrive for generations. In reality, the "story line" started in the early 1900s with her Ma Ma, Grandma Battaglia, and the recipes she left behind in the soon-to-be-famous brown leather-bound recipe book, crumbling after over a hundred years of use and abuse!

Acknowledgments

Life is a team sport, and the Warkenthien family is truly blessed to have a great team. Every member of our extended family: Dad, my ex-wife, Kim, Luann and Kurt—the other two siblings—and the nine grandkids all added significant threads to the tapestry. What emerged six months later is this work of love.

Taking it from the top: Reinhardt Warkenthien, my dad and the patriarch of the family, has been with Ma for over fifty-six years. It's more than just a cliché to say that none of us would have been here without their love and union. Quietly, he's the wizard behind the curtain, pulling the strings and keeping us all humming along. Dad, you play the most difficult of all musical instruments—the second fiddle—always allowing Ma to lead the band. I love you for that and will always strive to be like the father you've been for us kids.

Kim, my bride for twenty-four years following a courtship of two years before that, was always a favorite of the family. Even though we went our separate ways, I choose to cherish the memories we made together instead of mourning our time apart. You may not still be my wife, but you are still loved by all in the Warkenthien family—including me—and will never be forgotten. You were—and remain—the gold standard to which all sisters-in-law will always be measured. Thanks for your contribution to the cookbook. It meant a lot to us all.

Luann, my favorite sis, grew up squeezed between two Type A brothers, rarely enjoying the spotlight that Kurt and I always hogged. However, over the years, you found your voice, and you've become a beautiful, loving daughter, sister, mother, and aunt to our family. I can say with full certainty that without your massive efforts over the past several months, Ma's Cookbook would have never seen the shelf of any room. I can't begin to thank you for your contributions and coordination that pulled all this together—on time and under budget, by the way. What a project manager you are. ATTENTION: If any prospective employers are reading this, she'd be your best hire ever! Give her a ring—and then a job!

Kurt, my beloved kid brother (or Dr. Warkenthien to you) is an amazing individual. I have to say, however, that he's a lucky guy: He didn't have to make all his early major decisions by himself. You see, I chose to be a doctor when I was a kid (though I didn't follow through on that commitment), and Kurt decided to follow my career path. I decided to attend the University of Illinois, Champaign-Urbana, and he decided to do the same. In fact, I pledged the Delta Sigma Phi fraternity, and six years later, guess what, Kurt was a Delta Sig! Kurt sure made me stay on my toes as his older brother and self-assigned character builder to him and his sister. Fast forward to today, and you'll see Dr. Kurt operating a thriving practice—Golden Rule Family Practice Clinic, in Naperville, IL—one of the busiest in the State. Even more important, he has his priorities in the right place being the loving and doting father to his five kids. He lives his life for them, and I strive to be the father to my boys like Uncle Kurt. I love you, Bro.

Then there are nine—nine grandkids, that is. I want to thank every one of them for their "letters about Grandma" and favorite recipes, including My Three Sons (I'm kicking around a television show concept), Nick, Ross, and Will. Leading the charge of the cousins is Tony Stec, Luann's oldest, finest, and onliest (hey, anyone can pick a word from a dictionary. I choose to make some of mine up) child. Kurt's kids, Tricia, Stephanie (my Godchild), Reinhardt, Little Kurt, and D.J. all added their footprint to the landscape. Great letters, pictures, and recipes, all.

If you're curious about birth order, see the contents page, and it will be disclosed. Every one of the Gang of Nine poured their heart out to Grandma and made this book a very special gift. Uncle Jack loves you all.

REINHARDT

The Italianization of an American

I am an American of German decent, but after being married to Pauline and being part of a wonderful Italian family for fifty-six years, I have become very well Italianized. I remember meeting some of her cousins, and they asked me if I had any friends. I said I did, and they said to forget about them. I wouldn't have time for them. That turned out to be quite true. Meeting Pauline's grandmother Battaglia was an eye-opening experience. When I was introduced to her, she looked at me and said, "He's Medigan (meaning American), but that's OK—they're good, too." In an Italian family, you're either Italian or American.

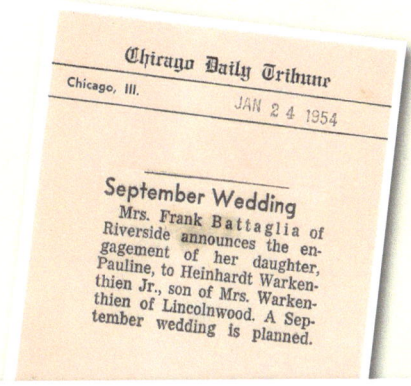

Chicago Daily Tribune

Chicago, Ill.   JAN 2 4 1954

September Wedding

Mrs. Frank Battaglia of Riverside announces the engagement of her daughter, Pauline, to Heinhardt Warkenthien Jr., son of Mrs. Warkenthien of Lincolnwood. A September wedding is planned.

My mother would cook typical American meat-and–potato dinners. Sunday dinner was at noon and cold-cut sandwiches about five in the evening. This gave us all Sunday afternoon to do what we wanted. Not in an Italian family. The main event of the day was dinner at three in the afternoon; nothing else mattered. The whole family gathered at my mother-in-law's house for Sunday dinner. I've always been a big eater, but those Sunday dinners were something.

My first experience at my future mother-in-law's for Sunday dinner was memorable. We all sat down, and out came the spaghetti and meatballs. I thought, *That's great, a good Italian spaghetti dinner.* I ate and stuffed myself; it was delicious. Then they cleared the table and brought out the main course: breaded veal cutlets. I had to force myself to eat more, but I did and loved it. With the Italians, spaghetti and meatballs are like an appetizer before the main meal.

Pauline and her sisters learned well from their mother. I've had many excellent dinners from Pauline's collection of recipes. To this day, our Sundays are very much the same spent with as many of our kids and grandkids as we can get together.

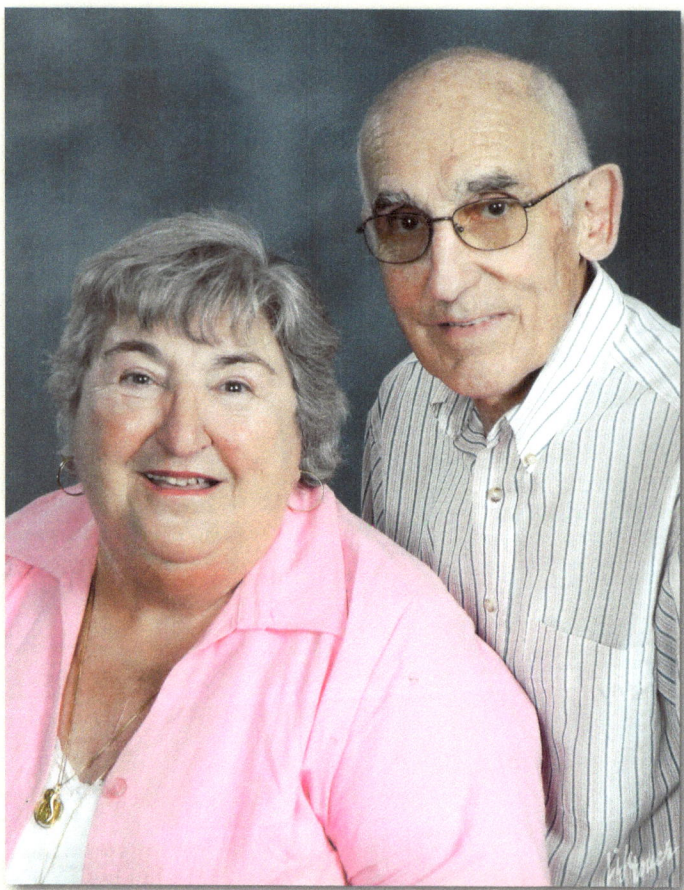

MaMa Portillo's Chocolate Cake

Ingredients

- 1 box Betty Crocker Super Moist Chocolate Butter Cake mix
- 3 large eggs
- 1 cup water
- 1 cup Hellman's mayo
- 2 cans Betty Crocker chocolate frosting

Directions

Preheat oven to 350 degrees. Beat all ingredients for 4 minutes. Pour into two greased round cake pans. Bake for 30 minutes. Cool completely. Frost with chocolate frosting.

Shrimp Scampi

Ingredients

1 lb raw shrimp, washed

2 tablespoons butter

1 tablespoon onion, minced

1 tablespoon olive oil

4 garlic cloves

1 tablespoon fresh lemon
   juice

Salt and pepper to taste

2 tablespoons fresh parsley

1 lb angel hair pasta, cooked

Romano cheese

Directions

Wash and de-vein shrimp; set aside. In a large frying pan, melt butter. Add onion, olive oil, cloves, lemon juice, salt, pepper, and parsley. Cook until bubbly. Add shrimp, stirring occasionally until shrimp turns pink. Serve over angel hair pasta topped with Romano cheese.

Veal Scaloppini (or Chicken)

Ingredients

2 lbs veal cutlets, ½-inch thick

1 clove garlic

¼ cup olive oil

1 15-oz can tomato sauce

½ teaspoon salt

1 teaspoon parsley, chopped

2 teaspoons black pepper

1 small can mushrooms

3 green peppers, chopped

1 lb pasta of choice, cooked

Directions

Brown cutlets, garlic, and olive oil in a frying pan. Combine tomato sauce, salt, parsley, black pepper, mushrooms, and green peppers, and pour into frying pan. Simmer for 1 hour until veal is tender. Serve with your pasta of choice.

Veal Marsala

Ingredients

2 lbs veal cutlets, ½-inch thick

1 clove garlic

¼ cup olive oil

¼ cup flour

Salt and pepper to taste

¼–½ cup marcella wine (white)

2 tablespoons parsley

¼ cup water

1 lb pasta of choice, cooked

Directions

Heat garlic and olive oil in a frying pan. Coat cutlets with flour, salt, and pepper. Brown cutlets on both sides in frying pan. While cutlets are browning, combine in bowl marcella wine, water, and parsley. Slowly add wine mixture over browned cutlets in frying pan. Simmer 20 minutes until veal is tender. If mixture gets too thick, add small amount of water. Serve over pasta of choice.

Italian Style Fried Chicken

Ingredients

1 frying chicken, 2–3 lbs

Olive oil; ½ inch deep in skillet

½ cup flour

1½ teaspoons salt

¼ teaspoon pepper

2 eggs, beaten

¼ cup milk

1 tablespoon parsley, chopped

½ cup parmesan cheese

1–2 tablespoons water

Directions

Clean and cut chicken into pieces. In a plastic bag, add flour, salt, and pepper. Shake 2 to 3 pieces of chicken into plastic bag, coat evenly. In a large bowl, combine eggs, milk, and parsley. Heat oil in skillet. When oil is heated, dip each piece of coated chicken in egg mixture. Roll chicken in parmesan cheese. Brown all sides of chicken in skillet. When chicken is evenly browned, reduce heat and add water. Cover tightly and cook slowly 25–40 minutes, until chicken is tender. Cook last 10 minutes uncovered.

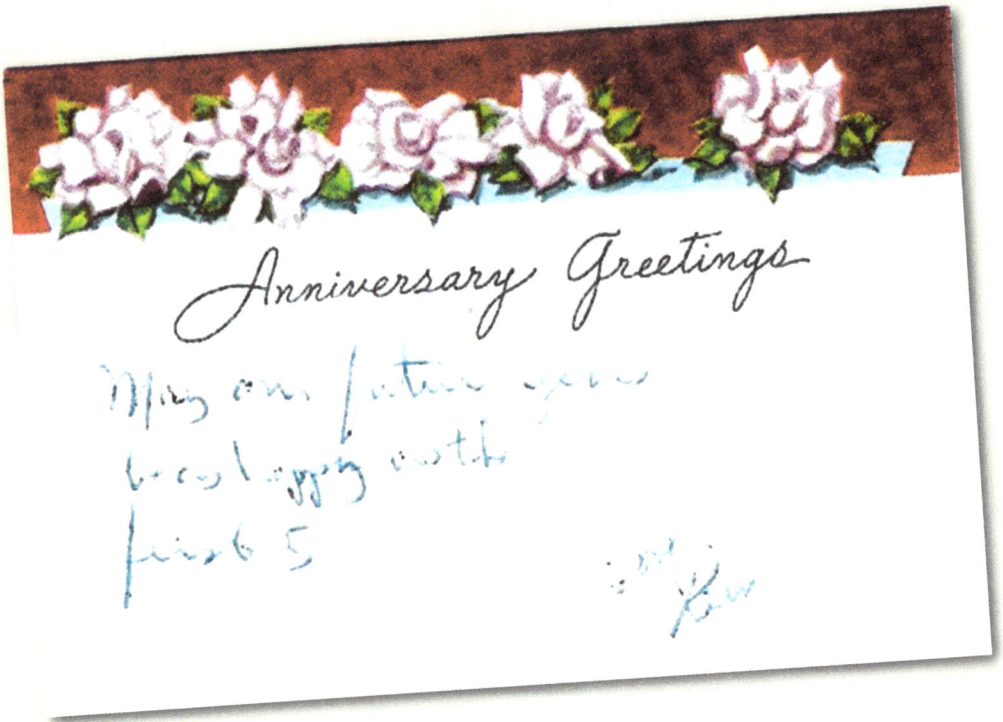

Anniversary Greetings

JACK

Ma's Language of Love
August 29, 2010

My Ma's a foodie. Some people eat to live while others live to eat. When you research the latter category, you're sure to see a picture of the Warkenthien family Matriarch. We are truly blessed because I know with certainty that she is the best (Italian) cook on the planet. I can't speak for the other solar systems. I'm personally at a huge disadvantage, however: I live in Texas, and everyone else in our extended family lives in Naperville, Illinois, making it really tough for me to drive in for Sunday afternoon dinners. Not to worry! Every time I jet into town, Ma prepares a few containers of gravy ready for me to carry back to Houston. I'm a master at boiling water and dropping in my favorite pasta for eleven minutes. There's been many a Sunday afternoon where I'll scare up a macaroni dinner for myself—and eat it at the same time as the family feasts over 1,200 miles away.

Of course, Ma and I talk several times a week. I'm never more than a phone conversation away from knowing exactly what she's either cooking or eating. I sense Dad sometimes gets tired of listening to the food "play-by-play" every time we chat. But I never do. Ever.

You see, food is my Ma's Language of Love—and I love her more in every way and every day of my life. God Bless you, Ma. I hope you cook for years to come because you're just hitting your stride!

Love,
JACK

Dearest Mom,

For Mother's Day, I decided to give you a little spending money. However, what you said the other night changed my mind. Seeing that you, instead, want me to take the money and put it in my college fund, I'll do that. Happy Mother's Day,

Lovingly, Jack

5-13-73

For fifty-four years—and running—I've enjoyed all of my Ma's culinary delights. Unfortunately, I haven't been around Ma and Dad's home on a daily basis since I graduated from Naperville Central High School over thirty-six years ago. From the time I attended the University of Illinois/Champaign-Urbana, I've been more of a dinner guest since I chose a profession that kept me moving around the country. However, I've been lucky over the years to visit home at least four to five times a year for a few nights. Therefore, every meal at home has to be carefully considered in advance.

To that end, the dishes that always make my short list include:

- Breaded pork/veal cutlets (don't forget the frausia!)
- Ravioli, with plenty of neck bones, (hot) Italian sausage and meatballs
- Artichokes—breaded with plenty of Italian seasoning
- Antipasto, in all its splendor
- Tossed Italian salad (some day, I will get the recipe for this masterpiece)
- Italian sausage sandwiches (don't forget the peppers and onions)

I could go on and on, but in all fairness, it's my right, obligation—and pleasure—to take Ma and Dad out to eat every time I'm in town. Otherwise, I'd be a selfish oldest son to be sure!

My Parents, My Inspiration

Antipasto Tray

Ingredients

2 tablespoons wine vinegar

3 tablespoons olive oil

1 tablespoon garlic powder

½ teaspoon salt (to taste)

½ teaspoon pepper

1 teaspoon oregano

2 celery stalks, chopped

1 jar green olives

1 can black olives

1 can artichoke hearts

1 lb broccoli tops, cooked

1 lb cauliflower tops, cooked

1 can artichoke hearts

¼ lb salami, cubed

½ lb provolone cheese, cubed

¼ lb pepperoni, cubed

Directions

In a bowl, combine wine vinegar, olive oil, garlic powder, salt, pepper, and oregano—set aside. Line a round tray with aluminum foil. Starting from the center working out, layer celery, black and green olives, broccoli tops, cauliflower tops, and artichoke hearts. On a toothpick, place rolled slice of salami, provolone cheese, and pepperoni. Pour combined liquid mixture over all. Chill until ready to serve.

Stuffed Artichokes

Ingredients

4 medium artichokes

1 teaspoon salt

⅔ cup bread crumbs

3 cloves garlic, sliced thin

1 teaspoon parmesan, grated

1 tablespoon parsley, chopped

1 teaspoon salt

¾ teaspoon pepper

2 cups water

2 tablespoons olive oil

Directions

Remove outside lower leaves and cut stems from washed artichokes. Mix together bread crumbs, garlic, parmesan, parsley, salt, and pepper. Stuff crumb mixture between leaves and over top of artichokes. Place artichokes in skillet with water. Sprinkle artichokes with olive oil. Cover and cook about 30 minutes or until leaves are tender. To eat artichokes, pull out leaves one by one and scrape with teeth.

Italian Salad Dressing

Ingredients

⅓ cup wine vinegar

½ teaspoon salt

½ teaspoon onion salt or fresh-cut onion

½ teaspoon garlic powder

½ teaspoon oregano

½ cup olive oil

Directions

Combine all ingredients. Pour over salad; mix with hands.

Italian Sausage with Peppers

Ingredients

2 lbs Italian sausage
4 bell peppers, sliced
1 onion, sliced
¼ cup olive oil
Italian bread

Directions

Preheat oven to 350 degrees. Put all ingredients in 13x9-inch baking pan; mix well and cover with foil. Bake 30 minutes; stir well. Bake additional 45 minutes. Serve on fresh Italian bread.

Veal or Pork Cutlets

Ingredients

2 lbs of veal or pork cutlets

2 eggs, scrambled

Bread crumbs

Olive oil

1 lb spaghetti, cooked
   (optional)

Directions

With wooden mallet, pound cutlets until flat. Dip cutlets into eggs and then bread crumbs, covering both sides of cutlets. Heat oil in frying pan. Over medium–high heat, brown both sides of cutlets. Serve alone or with spaghetti.

Kim

Ma Marks History with Food

To Pauline, affectionately known as "Ma," food is a love language. Her table is a place where family and friends gather, expect to enjoy a delicious meal and good company, and are never disappointed.

Ma is passionate about food, and she cooks with wild abandon. A good clean-up crew and willing taste-tester are a necessary part of the process. I am happy to oblige. On more occasions than not, I have humbly conceded my authority in my own kitchen to allow her to create her culinary masterpieces. Afterwards, while she basked in the glory of a fabulous meal, it was my turn to shine. I have been known to literally scrub gravy off the ceiling after she cooked in my kitchen. Really.

Ma marks history with food. Ask her about anything, and if there was a good meal involved, she will remember it. A conversation, an event, a celebration. She can tell you where we were, what she was wearing, and who was at the table on any given occasion if we were eating at the time. It could also be said that she makes history with food. She is solely responsible for a major grocery store chain in Texas carrying neck bones in their meat department.

Ma never met a stranger and exudes hospitality. Once, in the midst of my family's relocation across the country, she came to help us settle into the new house. Rather than unpacking moving boxes and hanging pictures on the wall, she was out meeting the new neighbors and inviting them to dinner. There's nothing quite like an impending dinner party to motivate one to set up housekeeping in record time. From that experience, I learned that welcoming friends and family around a dinner table is the most effective way to make a new house a home.

Ma creates memories with food. Whether it's Pizzagaina at Easter, Shrimp and Angel hair at the beach, or the aroma of her famous Red Sauce that I awoke to on many a Christmas Eve morning, many happy memories involve Ma's cooking. Food is her expression of love and her legacy.

Kim Warkenthien

Italian Easter Pie; Pizzagaina

Ingredients

3 lb ricotta cheese

½ cup Romano cheese

3 large eggs

3 tablespoons parsley

1 tablespoon garlic

½ lb salami, diced

½ lb pepperoni

1½ lb Italian sausage, cooked
and sliced

1 cup mozzarella cheese,
grated

Pastry dough

Directions

Preheat oven to 350 degrees. Mix all ingredients. Pour into a pastry dough lined 9x13-inch cake pan. Top with additional pastry dough. Brush with egg white. Bake for 45–60 minutes.

Note: A glass pan will give you a nice, browned crust.

Luann "Lu Lu"

Dinner Tonight Is . . .

Mom communicates clearly, directly, and often through her language of love:*food*. During our daily morning conversation she will always share with me her dinner menu, ending with an invite for me to join her and Daddy for dinner. To this day Green Bean Patties and her homemade Brochette are often way too hard to resist. My very first meal she taught me to cook was Chicken Versuvio. The best chicken marinate in the world is Mom's own Oil and Lemon. I assure you, it beats anything out there on the market. Whether it's cooking for the family or friends, no one will push away from the table not feeling full, and more times than not being entertained with her own special humor. No matter how hard I try to emulate her recipes, mine *never* taste as good as hers. Ma's philosophy is, if there's no leftovers then she didn't cook enough. At any time any of us can invite someone over to our family's home and Mom will be more then welcome to cook an authentic Italian feast. Mom shouts loud and clear her love for us all through her language of love:*food* Mom, I love you too!

Luann

Green Bean Patties

Ingredients

1 can green beans, drained

1 cup bread crumbs

½ cup parmesan cheese

4 eggs

Salt, pepper, and garlic
   powder to taste

Oil

Directions

In a bowl, combine all ingredients except oil. In skillet, heat oil. Mixing with a large spoon, pour ingredients into heated oil. Brown both sides.

To Mom
From LuLu

From Luam

Happy Mother's Day

I Hope it is hot Sunday

To you?

Brochette; Tomato and Mozzarella

Ingredients

3–4 ripe tomatoes, sliced
3–4 slices fresh mozzarella
Oregano
Garlic powder
Salt and pepper
Olive oil
Baguette toast, sliced

Directions

Arrange sliced tomatoes in overlapping pattern. Top with sliced mozzarella cheese. Sprinkle with oregano, garlic powder, salt, pepper, and olive oil. Serve over sliced baguette toast.

Chicken Vesuvio

Ingredients

1 whole chicken, cut into parts
½ cup olive oil
Salt and pepper to taste
1 small onion, chopped
1 teaspoon oregano
1 tablespoon parsley
1 clove garlic
Potatoes, cut and peeled (optional)

Directions

Preheat oven to 350 degrees. Mix all ingredients and put in covered roasting pan. Add optional potatoes. Bake for 1 hour covered. Uncover roasting pan; continue to bake until chicken turns brown.

Oil and Lemon Marinate

Ingredients

1 cup lemon juice
1 clove garlic
½ teaspoon oregano
½ cup olive oil
Salt and pepper to taste

Directions

In a large bowl, combine all ingredients. Add chicken or steak; let sit for 1 hour.

Italian Cookies—Biscotti

Ingredients

2 sticks margarine or butter
1½ cup sugar
6 eggs
2 teaspoons oil
4 cups sifted flour
4 tablespoons baking powder
½ teaspoon salt
½ teaspoon anise oil
Cocoa powder (optional)

Directions

Preheat oven to 350 degrees. Combine ingredients in large bowl; mix well. Form into three long stripes on cookie sheet. Bake until brown, about 20 minutes. Remove from oven and slice; increase oven heat to 400 degrees. Put back in oven for a couple minutes.

Pizzelle

Ingredients

12 eggs
2 cups sugar
2 cups oil
1 teaspoon pure anise oil
4 cups flour
Powdered sugar
Cocoa powder (optional)

Directions

Preheat Pizzelle maker. Beat eggs well; add sugar gradually and beat together. Add oil and anise oil; beat until blended smooth. Add flour a little at a time with optional cocoa powder; mix well. By spoonfuls, drop onto maker. Cook approximately 1 minute, until golden brown. Remove from maker; cool on flat surface. Sprinkle with powdered sugar before serving.

Angel Food Cake

Ingredients

1 box angel food cake mix
1 package chocolate frosting
1½ cups cold water

Directions

Preheat oven to 350 degrees. Beat cake mix and water on low speed 30 seconds; beat medium speed 1 minute. Pour into ungreased angel food cake pan. Bake 35–45 minutes or until top is dark golden brown. Immediately turn upside down onto glass bottle until cake is completely cool. Frost with chocolate frosting.

Kurt

Mail Delivery
September 8th, 2010

Mom's carrot cake arriving at the University of Illinois for my roommates and me is one of my fondest memories of college. When the mailman delivered the package, we all couldn't wait to eat the contents.

Kurt

TO THE BEST MOTHER EVER

Sometimes a boy is
Not so good
At saying all
The things he should.
But today is special,
So I want you to know--
You're the best mother ever.
And I love you so!

HAPPY
MOTHER'S DAY!

Kurt L.W.

Kurt has "dedicated" the doll house to him - with his name in large letters on the side. In order to help him learn to be responsible for this would you send some cleanser + an old rag + I'll have him at work on the damage tomorrow — thanks for taking over yesterday!

Stuffed Mushrooms

Ingredients

1 package large mushrooms
3 tablespoons butter
1 teaspoon garlic powder
Salt and pepper to taste
1 tablespoon parsley
1 egg
1 cup bread crumbs
Olive oil

Directions

Preheat oven to 350 degrees. Wash and remove stems from mushrooms. Chop stems into very small pieces. In frying pan, melt butter; add chopped stems, garlic powder, salt, pepper, parsley, egg, and bread crumbs. Add a little olive oil. Mix well. Stuff mushrooms with mixture. Bake in oven for 15–20 minutes.

Carrot Cake

Ingredients

4 eggs
1½ cups sugar
1½ cups Wesson oil
3 cups flour
2 teaspoons baking powder
2 teaspoons baking soda
2 teaspoons cinnamon
1 teaspoon salt
2 cups carrots, grated
1 cup pineapple, crushed
½–¾ cups nuts, chopped

Directions

Preheat oven to 350 degrees. Mix all ingredients. Pour into greased angel food cake pan. Bake 75 minutes.

Tony "Tony Bob"

Not So Much the Love of Food as Much as it is the Food of Love

When I think of my grandma, two words come to mind: love and food. It's not so much the love of food as much as it is the food of love. Food isn't just food in our family, food is what makes us a family. It's how my Grandma shows us she loves us. Most of my memories from growing up with Grandma have food in them somewhere, and I'm sure we'll have many more just like them.

When I was in grade school and Christmas was coming, most kids were just waiting for the day school got out so they could sit at home and spend their time searching for gifts in their houses. Little did they know that there'd be a day coming very soon when they would have to wake up early and go to school while my grandma would keep me home with her just to bake all of our Christmas cookies. Every year she'd make sure that I helped with the mixing and the shaping and the baking and—most importantly—with the eating of the cookies. And man, did I eat those spritzers. Especially the green ones; everyone knows they are way better than all the other colors. Not to mention that I didn't need any extra time searching for presents—I knew where grandma hid them all anyway (just like I still know where all the change jugs are).

Grandma and I have always had a special relationship. It's probably because I was with her everyday, but I think it's because she likes me the best. I am the only one who can really yell back at her (even though when I do, she may just throw something in my direction), and who else could she chase around the house with a wooden spoon and laugh about it later? (You know how I get even? I just step on her oxygen hose . . .)

Christmas Eve is the big day. I mean yeah, it's nice and all that Uncle Jack and the boys come in, but it's when Grandma really goes all out. The day starts with baked clams, fried smelts, antipasto plates, and salad and ends with lobster tail, pasta with calamari sauce, and dessert. Can't beat that.

Senior year of high school, I wanted to have my football team over for dinner. Grandma shared the love with the whole team. She cooked pasta, meatballs, sausage, and peppers, all the good stuff for a very big group of growing boys . . . needless to say, not one of them left her house hungry.

One thing of Gram's I've always loved is her jelly. I can always find a few jars in the basement and snag the best ones to bring home: strawberry and apricot.

To this day, nothing beats going over to Grandma's house, raiding the refrigerator, watching the Cubs game, and sitting at the dinner table with the family. OK, maybe one thing beats it; my absolute favorite food of Grandma's has to be her veal cutlets. If those are there, then it's a good day. I could eat them all day. They just never get old. What's better than veal breaded and fried? Even if they are really pork....

So all of these years when we thought Grandma was just cooking and cooking and cooking (and cooking and cooking and cooking) because that's just what Italian grandmothers did, we didn't really realize why she did it. Food is part of what keeps our family close. It's the common denominator that will never change for us because of Grandma. As we get older and time gets in the way, food is what will bring our family together and what always has . . . and it's always her that makes it all happen. Now we know: she cooks because she loves us.

Now it's my turn to tell you, I love you, too, Grandma.

Tony

CHRISTMAS COOKIES

Ingredients

1 cup butter

⅔ cup sugar

3 egg yolks

1 teaspoon vanilla

2½ cups flour

Food coloring (optional)

Directions

Preheat oven to 400 degrees. Combine in mixer butter, sugar, yolks, and vanilla. Mix in flour. Optionally, divide dough and add food coloring. Cookie press dough onto cookie sheet; bake for 10 minutes.

PEPPERONI BREAD

Ingredients

2 loaves frozen bread dough

1 stick pepperoni, sliced and divided

2 cups mozzarella cheese, divided

Garlic powder

Salt and pepper to taste

1 egg white

Directions

Preheat oven to 375 degrees. Thaw bread dough and let rise according to package directions. Punch down and roll into rectangle on a floured surface. Sprinkle with cheese, seasonings, and pepperoni. Roll bread into loaf and place on greased cookie sheet, seam side down. Brush with egg white. Bake for 30–35 minutes until golden brown.

Nick
Nickelodeon–"Lode"
Better than Dining at Any Restaurant on Michigan Ave

I wish everybody could experience a dinner prepared by Grandma Warkenthien. Her world seems to revolve around what is going to be on the table for the evening because it surely means she'll be surrounded by family. No matter what day, what time, it is always going to be Italian, and always going to taste amazing. I can count on it.

It is such a treat to be able to take my girlfriends out of Chicago and out to dinner at my grandma's. Hands down, it will be better than dining at any restaurant on Michigan Avenue. There will always be a gigantic bowl of pasta, tons of meatballs, and a delectable salad for eating after. Add in great company, conversation, and an evening full of belly laughs from Grandma, and you have a dinner that won't soon be forgotten.

One time I ate so much that I literally fell asleep, face first, into my spaghetti. Her pasta bowls are classic, and you won't find more authentic, better-tasting pasta around.

There is one night out of the year that I wouldn't miss for the world. The Christmas Eve seafood feast. Starting at noon the day before Christmas, the tables are filled with everything from shrimp, clams, and scallops, to smelts and galamad, all topped off with a buttery lobster tail. By the end of the evening, I'm without a care in the world, butter dripping down my elbows, and the guests can barely get out of their chairs to get ready for mass.

The point is, my grandma is the best Italian cook I know. I will always look forward to dinnertime at the grandparents'. I know I'll never be disappointed, not once, not never.

By Nick Warkenthien

Ross

100 Meatballs

For as long as I can remember, every time I have gone to Chicago I look forward to one thing most—or, in this case, a hundred things. Meatballs! Handmade Italian meatballs, to be exact. When I was younger, I boldly proclaimed that I could eat "a hundred" of Grandma's meatballs. Since then, every time we visited for the holidays, I could count on getting more than my fair share of them.

But Grandma's excellence in the kitchen doesn't just end at her original, out-of-this-world meatballs. Homemade raviolis as big as a dinner plate make my mouth water just thinking about them. Veal cutlets (if there are any left after my dad gets into them) satisfy my hunger no matter what I'm hungry for. Most kids look forward to presents and stockings on Christmas. While I do, too, the thing I look forward to most every Christmas is the succulent seafood smorgasbord. Smelts, clams, shrimp, fish, calamari, and lobster are on the menu every Christmas Eve. That has remained unchanged for as long as I can remember.

When I think of good food, I think of Grandma. All the five-star restaurants in the world don't come close to the masterpieces I've seen my Grandma prepare in her kitchen.

Ross Warkenthien

Italian Meatballs

Ingredients

1 lb ground beef

½ lb ground pork

½ cup bread crumbs

2 tablespoons parmesan cheese

1 tablespoon parsley

1 egg

Salt and pepper to taste

1 lb pasta of choice, cooked

Directions

In a bowl, combine all ingredients. Shape into 1–2 inch balls. Brown in frying pan. When browned, put in Italian tomato sauce and cook. Serve with your favorite pasta.

TRICIA

A Slice of Tropical Paradise

Grandmas pineapple upside down cake has always been a favorite of mine. From the gooey sugary glaze to the moist, spongey center, every bite is an explosion of pineapple, fruity goodness. She starts out by making the yellow cake in the mold and then mixes up the brown sugar glaze so that there is a crystalized sugar crust and then finally all gets tied together with big golden slices of pineapple with plump red cherries on top. The first time she made it, I was intrigued to know why its called "upside down" cake, its gets this off beat name from the way you make it. You put the yellow cake mold upside down in the oven and then when its ready, you flip it back right side up, this gives it a uniqueness to it. Every birthday since I can remember, I don't ask for any other cake, because no other cake can stand a chance against this slice of tropical paradise. Each piece melts in your mouth with every bite, leaving you want more and more. Its the perfect cake for a summer birthday, and this is one cake that will always be in style. This cake is just one more little thing about my grandma that makes her such an amazing chef!

Love you grandma,
Tricia

Pineapple Upside-Down Cake

Ingredients

½ cup butter or margarine

1 packed cup brown sugar

1 20-oz can pineapple slices, undrained

10 maraschino cherries, drained

½ cup nuts, chopped

1 yellow cake mix

3 eggs

½ cup vegetable oil

1 cup thawed, frozen whipped topping

Directions

Preheat oven to 350 degrees. Melt butter in 12-inch skillet over low heat. Remove from heat, stir in brown sugar until well blended. Drain pineapple, reserving juice; set aside. Arrange pineapple slices over brown sugar mixture in skillet. Place a cherry in center of each pineapple slice. Sprinkle with nuts. Add enough water to pineapple juice to measure 1⅓ cups liquid. Combine cake mix, pineapple juice, eggs, and oil until well blended and smooth. Pour over fruit mixture in skillet. Bake 35–40 minutes or until wooden pick inserted in center comes out clean. Remove from oven, cool 5 minutes. Carefully loosen edges of cake. Invert onto large serving plate. Cool slightly, garnish with whipped topping.

WILL "DIPPER"

Brings the Whole Family Together

Grandma's cooking has always been my favorite thing about going to Chicago. I can always count on an amazing meal right when I get there. Whether she's cooking up veal cutlets or spaghetti and meatballs, it's impossible to say which food is my favorite.

But I think the thing I enjoy the most is how it brings the whole family together. No matter if it's Italian sausages, lobster, ravioli, or her delicious salads, we all gather around the same table at the end of the day. My grandma is one of the best cooks I know, and through her cooking she brings the whole family together.

WILL WARKENTHIEN

Veal Parmesan (or pork)

Ingredients

2 lbs veal cutlets, ½-inch thick

1½ cups fine bread crumbs

½ cup parmesan cheese, grated

3 beaten eggs

1 teaspoon salt

¼ teaspoon pepper

½ cup olive oil

2 cups tomato sauce

2 cups mozzarella cheese, shredded

Directions

Preheat oven to 350 degrees. Mix bread crumbs and parmesan cheese. Combine eggs, salt, and pepper. Heat olive oil in skillet. Dip cutlets into egg mixture and then into bread crumbs, covering both sides. Add cutlets to skillet and brown on both sides. Arrange cutlets in baking dish. Pour tomato sauce over cutlets. Top cutlets with mozzarella cheese. Bake 15–20 minutes or until cheese is melted.

Stephanie

Always Made with Enough Love to Fill a Room

Anytime I think of Grandma's house, food is always the first thing that comes to my mind! So of course, any favorite memory of Grandma is a food memory or an instant recipe that pops into my mind. By far my favorite memory/food memory of Grandma is Christmas dinner—especially Christmas dinner when I was a kid. The smell of three different courses cooking all at once as you walk in the door, and the joy of cousins running up to give you hugs, is unbeatable. My favorite part has to be the appetizer of all-you-can-eat shrimp and the main course of pounds of pasta and meat and almost every carbohydrate you could think of (a runner's dream). Then dessert comes out, and it just gets better: homemade cookies, cheesecake, pie, too many sweets to handle. But the best of the best are the homemade pitzzels! After working over a hot griddle all day, putting powdered sugar on every individual one and even with a choice of chocolate or original flavors, they are so delicious and amazing that they don't even taste the same if they're not made by Grandma's hands. Anything that is made by Grandma is awesome and delectable every time. Her food is always made with enough love to fill a room, and it is one of the biggest things I miss being away at college all year long!

I LOVE YOU, GRANDMA, A&F

Steph

Baked Mastaccoli

Ingredients

1 lb mastaccoli or rigatoni,
  cooked and drained

Base Italian sauce

1 cup shredded mozzarella
  cheese

Directions

Preheat oven to 325 degrees. Mix pasta with sauce, then pour into 13x9-inch baking pan. Top with mozzarella cheese. Bake until cheese melts, approximately 30 minutes.

REINHARDT

I'm Always Able to Have Her in My Mind and Heart

My grandma's great Ravioli.
I would always remember my grand mothers way of making raviolli. she would always make it for my Birthday, and she would always show me how, with guidance and with Love. There was always enough Ravioli for dinner and yet still we alway had extras. she would also give me guidence and knowledge from her past to entertain me. And that is why her raviolli always remynds me of her and her unending Love. I am Learning how to cook from her, and already know how to make Basteiz Pasta, and teaching me how to make her pasta gravy. through this I can always be able to have her in my mind and heart. I love my grandma

Bastine

Ingredients

1 lb box bastine
4 quarts water
¼ cup butter
2 eggs

Directions

In a medium sauce pan, bring water to boil; add bastine. Cook until tender; drain. Pour back into saucepan and add butter and eggs. Cook until butter melts and eggs are cooked. Stir frequently.

Garlic Bread

Ingredients

1 loaf Italian bread, cut in half
    lengthwise
1 stick butter, melted
Garlic powder
¾ cup Romano cheese
½ teaspoon of paprika

Directions

Preheat oven to 425 degrees. Mix melted butter, garlic powder, Romano cheese, and paprika in a bowl. Spread mixture on bread; bake until crisp and brown.

Ravioli

Ingredients

1 lb ravioli
6 quarts water
1 teaspoon salt
Spaghetti sauce, heated
Parmesan or Romano cheese

Directions

In a large saucepan, add water and salt; bring to rapid boil. Add ravioli and cook until tender and floating on surface of water. Drain well. Layer on large platter, starting with sauce. Sprinkle top with cheese.

LITTLE KURT

It's Not Sauce, it's Gravy

One of my favorite foods that grandma makes is her neckbone + gravy combo. At almost every sphaghetti meal grandma makes this delicious cumbo. She cooks the neckbones perfectly to where the meat almost falls off the bone. Then the gravy, oh my god the gravy is amazing! She always told me that it is not sauce, its gravy. The gravy just compliments the neckbones in such a way that it makes them irresistable. But the neckbones have a certian taste to them unlike any other meat I have had. That is why I love them. I also love to cook them with her because every time she tells a little bit more on how to make her gravy. Some day I will maybe make the gravy like her one day. She also adds the littlest details to the meal that makes the biggest diffrence. But usually when she annances that they are done cooking we all run into the kitchen fight over the bigget piece until I finally get that savory, irresistable and decadent piece of neckbone and gravy, that she cooks with love every time.

Kurt W.
♡ luv u g-ma!

Base Italian Sauce with Neck Bones

Ingredients

1 lb pork neck bones
Base Italian sauce

Directions

Add neck bones and brown with additional ingredients. Serve along with meatballs in the Italian sauce.

Note: See page 44 for Italian Sausage recipe.

D. J.

The Smell Hits You Like a Punch from Tyson

One memory that i have with my grandma and cooking is her famous monkey Bread. My grandma makes the best monkey bread because she puts a twist in it by adding a sugary glaze. Whenever im sick my grandma always makes me her monkey bread or i go over to her house and make it with her. I really enjoy making it with her because it always finds a way to cheer me up because my grandma has that look and joy when she cooks with me. I also love this dessert because it takes her no time to make it, and I keep learning on how to cook it like her. The smell hits you like a punch from mike Tyson when you walk into the front door. Then when you walk into the kitchen you see the 2 circles off monkey bread the one that she keeps for herself and grenpa, and the other one that me and my siblings share. Of course I have the most out of everybody. Then after about 3 minutes me and my brothers fight for the last piece, that usualy tastes the best because it's the one that you savor the most

D.J. Warkenthien

Monkey Bread

Ingredients

4 cans biscuits
⅔ cup sugar
1 tablespoon cinnamon
½ cup butter
1 cup brown sugar
1 teaspoon cinnamon

Directions

Preheat oven to 350 degrees. Tear apart biscuits. Put biscuits, sugar, and cinnamon in bag; shake well. Place covered biscuits in greased angel food pan. Mix in bowl butter, brown sugar, and additional cinnamon. Pour on top of biscuits. Bake 30 minutes. Immediately remove biscuits from pan by inverting onto platter.

Ma's Favorites

Her Language of Love: Food

Asparagus Romano

Ingredients

Ingredients
2 lbs asparagus, fresh
¼ stick butter, melted
1 cup bread crumbs
¼ cup Romano cheese
1 clove garlic
¼ teaspoon oregano
¼ teaspoon basil
2 tablespoons butter, melted

Directions

Preheat oven to 350 degrees. Wash asparagus and cut off tough ends. Cook for 5 minutes. Arrange asparagus in baking pan; baste with melted butter. Mix bread crumbs, Romano cheese, garlic, oregano, and basil with 2 tablespoons of melted butter. Spread over asparagus. Bake 20 minutes or until browned.

Base Recipe for Italian Sauce

Ingredients

¼ cup olive oil

1 onion, chopped

2-3 lbs pork ribs or 1-2 lbs
    neck bones

1 tablespoon parsley

1 tablespoon salt

1 tablespoon pepper

1 bay leaf

2 cloves of garlic

2 28-oz cans tomato sauce

Directions

In a large sauce pan, combine all ingredients except tomato sauce. Brown, turning occasionally. Add cans of tomato sauce and simmer uncovered over low heat. Stirring occasionally, cook about 3 hours. If sauce becomes too thick, add ½ cup water.

Note: Add 1 lb of Italian sausage and brown with additional ingredients to make Base Itialian Sauce with Sausage.

Chicken Cacciatore

Ingredients

2–3 lbs chicken parts

½ cup olive oil

2 cloves garlic

1 15-oz can tomatoes

½ cup white wine

Salt and pepper to taste

1 tablespoon oregano

Cooked noodles

1 small can mushrooms
 (optional)

1 green pepper, chopped
 (optional)

1 small onion, chopped
 (optional)

Directions

In a frying pan, brown chicken on both sides in olive oil and garlic. Combine in a bowl tomatoes, white wine, salt, pepper, and oregano. Slowly pour mixture over chicken in frying pan. Simmer slowly for 30 minutes. Optionally, add mushrooms, green pepper, and onion. If sauce gets too thick, add a little water. Serve over cooked noodles.

Easy Beef Stroganoff

Ingredients

2 lbs round steak, cut into
 strips

5 tablespoons flour

Salt and pepper to taste

½ onion, chopped

1 clove garlic

3 tablespoons shortening

1 cup sour cream

½ cup catsup

1 cup water

1 lb egg noodles, cooked

Directions

Shake in a paper bag: flour, salt, and pepper. Brown meat, onions, and garlic in shortening. In bowl, combine sour cream, catsup, and water. Pour over meat. Simmer covered for about 90 minutes. Stir occasionally. Serve over hot noodles.

Light Italian Casserole

Ingredients

1½ lb ground beef

1 package Italian dry salami

1 green pepper, chopped

2 cloves garlic

1 onion, chopped

1 14-oz can diced undrained
  tomatoes

1 6½-oz can drained
  mushrooms

1 tablespoon Italian
  seasoning

1 teaspoon oregano

Salt and pepper to taste

½ lb cooked spaghetti

8 oz mozzarella cheese,
  shredded

Directions

Preheat oven to 325 degrees. In a skillet, cook ground beef, salami, green pepper, garlic, and onion until meat is no longer pink. Stir in tomatoes, mushrooms, Italian seasoning, oregano, salt, pepper, and cooked spaghetti. Spaghetti should be broken in half prior to being cooked. Spread mixture in a 13x9-inch pan sprayed with non-stick spray oil. Top with mozzarella cheese. Bake until hot and bubbly, 45–50 minutes.

Quick Italian Cake

Ingredients

2 cups flour
3 tablespoons sugar
½ teaspoon salt
2½ teaspoons baking powder
4 tablespoons softened butter
1 cup milk
1 teaspoon rum

Directions

Preheat oven to 325 degrees. Stir dry ingredients together with softened butter. Add milk and stir until batter is stiff. Spread batter in 8x8 baking dish. Bake for 25 minutes.

Italian Butter Cookies

Ingredients

½ lb butter
2 tablespoons vanilla
¼ teaspoon anise oil
2 cups flour
½ cup ground walnuts
2 tablespoons powdered sugar

Directions

Preheat oven to 350 degrees. Mix butter, vanilla, anise oil, flour, and walnuts. Roll into balls; flatten slightly and place on cookie sheet. Bake for 15 minutes or until brown. Roll in powdered sugar.

Italian Pound Cake

Ingredients

1 lb margarine
1 lb powdered sugar
1 lb cake flour
1 teaspoon vanilla
¼ teaspoon anise oil

Directions

Preheat oven to 350 degrees. Combine all ingredients; pour into a greased loaf pan. Bake for 60 minutes.

Italian Cookies

Ingredients

2 sticks butter or margarine

1½ cup sugar

6 eggs

2 teaspoons oil

4 cups sifted flour

4 teaspoons baking powder

½ teaspoon salt

½ teaspoon anise oil

Directions

Preheat oven to 400 degrees. Mix all ingredients well. Form into 3-inch long strips; place on cookie sheet. Bake 20 minutes or until brown. Remove from oven and slice.

Hearty Barley Soup

Ingredients

½ lb lean ground beef

½ cup onion, chopped

1 clove garlic, minced

7 cups water

1 14½-oz can tomatoes, cut in pieces

½ cup medium Quaker Barley, uncooked

½ cup celery, sliced

½ cup carrots, sliced

2 beef bouillon cubes

½ teaspoon dried basil, crushed

1 bay leaf

1 9-oz package frozen vegetables

Directions

In a 4-quart saucepan, brown meat. Add onion and garlic; cook until onion is tender. Drain. Stir in remaining ingredients—except for frozen vegetables. Cover and bring to a boil. Reduce heat and simmer 50–60 minutes, stirring occasionally. Add frozen vegetables; cook about 10 minutes or until vegetables are tender. Additional water may be added if soup becomes too thick.

Italian Wedding Soup

Ingredients

2 lbs ground beef

¾ cup bread crumbs

1 teaspoon parsley

1 teaspoon garlic powder

Salt and pepper to taste

2 eggs

4 cups clear chicken broth

2 bunches escarole

Romano cheese

½ lb angel hair pasta, cooked (optional)

Directions

Mix ground beef, bread crumbs, parsley, garlic powder, salt, pepper, and eggs. Shape into little balls. In a kettle, cook escarole in chicken broth until tender. Add little balls to soup; cook until boiling. Simmer 10 minutes. Optionally, cook angel hair. Serve in bowls sprinkled with Romano cheese.

Lasagna

Ingredients

1 lb lasagna noodles, cooked

¾ lb mozzarella cheese, sliced

¼ cup parmesan cheese, grated

½ teaspoon pepper

1 cup ricotta cheese

Tomato meat sauce

Directions

Preheat oven to 350 degrees. Drain cooked noodles well. Pour ½ cup of tomato sauce into baking dish. Top with layer of noodles (about ⅓ of noodles) and ½ of mozzarella cheese. Sprinkle with ½ of parmesan cheese and pepper. Top with ½ of ricotta cheese. Beginning with sauce, repeat layering, ending with ricotta cheese. Top with more sauce. Bake about 30 minutes or until mixture is bubbling.

Marinara Sauce (meatless sauce)

Ingredients

½ cup olive oil
2 cloves garlic
1¼ teaspoons of salt
1 teaspoon of pepper
1 tablespoon of parsley, chopped
1 28-oz can of tomato sauce
Cooked pasta of choice
Romano cheese

Directions

Brown olive oil, garlic, salt, pepper, and parsley for approximately 5 minutes. Slowly add tomato sauce. Cook rapidly; stir occasionally for approximately 15 minutes or until sauce thickens. Serve over pasta; sprinkle with Romano cheese.

Garlic Sauce

Ingredients

¾ cup of butter
2 gloves garlic (don't be afraid to use more)
1 teaspoon parsley, chopped
2 cups water
1 lb thin spaghetti, cooked
Grated cheese

Directions

Mix all ingredients in sauce pan; cook approximately 10 minutes. Serve over spaghetti. Sprinkle with cheese.

Olive Oil and Garlic Sauce

Ingredients

½ cup olive oil
4 cloves garlic, chopped
¾ cups water
Salt and pepper to taste
1 teaspoon parsley
1 lb spaghetti, cooked
Romano cheese

Directions

Brown olive oil and garlic; add water, salt, pepper, and parsley. Cook approximately 10 minutes. Serve over spaghetti. Sprinkle with cheese.

Pasta with Broccoli

Ingredients

1½ lbs broccoli

½ cup olive oil

2–3 cloves garlic

Salt and pepper to taste

3 cups water

1 lb macaroni of choice , cooked

Romano cheese

Directions

Bring water to boil; add broccoli. Cook broccoli until tender; drain water. Add olive oil, garlic, salt, and pepper. Serve with macaroni or spaghetti. Sprinkle with Romano cheese.

Omelet (Frittata)

Ingredients

6 eggs

½ cup milk

Salt and pepper to taste

Bread crumbs

3 tablespoons olive oil

Romano cheese

Garlic powder

Basil

Vegetables of choice, cooked (optional)

Sausage (optional)

Directions

In a bowl, scramble eggs with milk. Add salt, pepper, and bread crumbs. Add olive oil to 9-inch frying pan. Pour egg mixture into heated frying pan. When it starts to crust on the side, add Romano cheese, garlic powder, and basil. Optionally, add vegetables and sausage. Turn over; cook on other side.

Chicken with Artichokes and Mushrooms

Ingredients

6 chicken breasts
1 cup flour
Salt and pepper to taste
½ cup olive oil
1 onion, chopped
1 can mushrooms
1 can artichokes
½ cup white wine
1 cup chicken broth
1 lb angel hair pasta, cooked

Directions

Dip chicken breasts in flour, salt, and pepper. Add oil to frying pan; brown both sides of chicken. Stir in onion, mushrooms, artichokes, wine, and broth. Cover pan and cook 30 minutes. Serve over pasta.

Eggplant Parmesan

Ingredients

1 eggplant of at least 1 lb, peeled and sliced
2 eggs, slightly beaten
¼ cup milk
3 tablespoons olive oil
⅔ cup bread crumbs
1 cup parmesan cheese, grated
3 ounces mozzarella cheese, shredded
2 cups tomato sauce

Directions

Preheat oven to 350 degrees. In skillet, heat olive oil. In bowl, combine eggs and milk. Dip eggplant in egg mixture, then bread crumbs. Brown both sides in skillet. Pour 1 cup tomato sauce in bottom of casserole dish. Layer with ½ eggplant and ½ cup parmesan cheese. Repeat layers, ending with mozzarella cheese. Bake about 20 minutes or until cheese is melted.

Saint Joseph's Day Cream Puffs

Ingredients

1 cup hot water
½ cup butter
1 tablespoon sugar
½ teaspoon salt
1 cup flour
4 eggs

Directions

Preheat oven to 350 degrees. In saucepan, bring to boil water, butter, sugar, and salt. After mixture starts to boil, add flour. Beat vigorously with wooden spoon until mixture leaves sides of pan and forms a smooth ball, approximately 3 minutes. Remove from heat. Quickly beat eggs in one at a time until batter is smooth and glossy. Drop by tablespoons 2 inches apart onto baking sheet. Bake 15 minutes. Remove from pan, slit one side, cool completely. After cooled, cut puff in half. Fill bottom half with filling. Place top half back onto puff.

Filling

Ingredients

3 cups ricotta cheese
1 teaspoon vanilla
2 tablespoons orange peel, grated
1 cup chocolate chips
1 tablespoon sugar

Directions

Mix all ingredients in a blender at low speed.

Linguine with White Clam Sauce

Ingredients

3 tablespoons virgin olive oil

3 cloves garlic

1 8-oz bottle clam juice

2 cups water

Salt and pepper to taste

½ onion, chopped

1 tablespoon parsley

2 cans clams

1 lb linguine, cooked

Romano cheese

Directions

Combine olive oil, garlic, clam juice, water, salt, pepper, onions, and parsley. Cook for 3 minutes until boiling. Just before serving, add clams. Serve over linguine. Top with cheese.

Uncooked Tomato Sauce

Ingredients

4–5 tomatoes, cut into small
   pieces

1 clove garlic, pressed

3 tablespoons olive oil

1 teaspoon salt

Pepper to taste

½ lb pasta, cooked

Cheese, grated

4 basil leaves, chopped

Directions

Mix all ingredients in bowl; let stand at room temperature for one hour. Serve over cooked pasta and grated cheese.

Dearies,
We all had a velly, velly VELLY grand and wonderful time at your home on Saturday! Mmmmm!!! That Italian dinner you served was ARE delicious!!! YOUR MOM surely does make the RAVIOLI!!! Thank you for ALL the hours that went into the preparation of this SUPER MEAL!!! We enjoyed your smallfry too. Jackie is quite the guitar player — Lulu is a mighty fine little LADY and YOUR WEE KURT is a clown of the FIRST degree. All 3 have such boundless energy. We envy them! God love you one & all! Gratefully, All the Sisters of St. Andrews!

Quick Tomato Sauce

Ingredients

1 lb ground beef, browned
1 cup bread crumbs
1 tablespoon garlic salt
1 teaspoon parsley
1 egg
1 28-oz can tomato sauce

Directions

Mix ground beef, bread crumbs, garlic salt, parsley, and egg. Add tomato sauce. In saucepan, cook for 1 hour.

Italian Cheesecake

Ingredients

3 packages cream cheese,
    4-oz each

2 eggs, beaten

¾ cups sugar

2 tablespoons vanilla

½ teaspoon lemon juice

Directions

Preheat oven to 350 degrees. Combine all ingredients; beat until light and fluffy. Pour onto graham cracker crust. Bake for 20 minutes. After cooled, top with topping. Put back into oven for 10 minutes. Cool and serve.

Crust

Ingredients

15 graham crackers, crushed

¼ cup sugar

¼ cup melted butter

Directions

Combine all ingredients, press down into bottom of 9-inch cake pan.

Topping

Ingredients

1 cup sour cream

¾ cup sugar

1 teaspoon vanilla

Directions

Combine all ingredients.

Sour Cream Coffee Cake

Ingredients

1 stick butter
1 cup sugar
2 eggs
1 teaspoon vanilla
2 cups flour
1 teaspoon baking soda
1 cup sour cream
½ cup walnuts, chopped
¾ cup brown sugar
1 tablespoon cinnamon
Powdered sugar

Directions

Preheat oven to 350 degrees. Mix butter, sugar, eggs, vanilla, flour, baking soda, and sour cream. Pour ½ dough into greased angel food cake pan. Combine walnuts, brown sugar, and cinnamon. Sprinkle ½ of topping mixture over dough. Put remaining dough in pan and top with remaining topping. Bake for 45 minutes. Turn upside down as soon as cooled. Sprinkle with powdered sugar.

Zucchini Bread

Ingredients

3 eggs
1 cup oil
2 cups sugar
2 cups zucchini, shredded
3 teaspoons vanilla
3 cups flour
1 teaspoon salt
3 teaspoons cinnamon
½ teaspoon baking powder

Directions

Preheat oven to 325 degrees. In a large bowl, mix together eggs, oil, sugar, zucchini, and vanilla. Stir in flour, salt, cinnamon, and baking powder. Pour into 2 greased and floured bread pans. Bake for 1 hour.

Chili

Ingredients

1 medium onion, chopped

1 lb ground beef

2 cans chili beans

1 can tomato sauce

1 pkg frozen tamales (optional)

Cheese, shredded (optional)

Crackers (optional)

Directions

In a skillet, brown onion and ground beef. Transfer to large sauce pan; add chili beans and tomato sauce. Add additional seasoning if desired. Heat over low temperature, stirring occasionally. Serve with toppings of choice.

GRANDMA BATTAGLIA

"Ma Ma" —Anna Battaglia

ORIGINAL HANDWRITTEN RECIPES FROM THE EARLY 1900S

Oct. 14, 1912.

Picalli.

1 head cabbage
1 pk green tomatoes
6 stalk celery
1 doz onions
1 T celery seed
1 T sugar
3 red
    or } peppers.
green }

6 green
1 doz cucumber
? vinegar to cover
? salt to taste.

Method:

Wash all vegeta
carefully. Chop all
very fine and sa
over night. Drain
carefully. Boil
vinegar, sugar a
spices about 5 mi
add the chop
vegetables and
boil about 5 mi
put into sterili
jars. Seal secure

Apple Sauce

1 = 1 apple   Method: Wash wipe
1 c = 1 T sugar   core & pare apples make
1 c = ½ c water.   syrup by boiling
sugar and water 5 min cook until
very soft. with a fork until the sauce
is flaky. A slice of lemon may be
added with cooking.

Spiced Apple Sauce.

1½ ground spices.

1 T - 1 apple

1 c - 1 T sugar.

1 c - ½ c water

Method.

Wash wipe core & apple make, syrup by boiling sugar & water for 5 min. Cook until soft with a fork wipe the fork until the sauce is very flaky,

Catsup

54 tomatoes

6 peppers

2 onions

1 T salt

2 c sugar

4 c vinegar

⅛ t cinnamon (or allspice and bay

Baked Apples.

Apples.
½ c Sugar 2 T
¼ T cinnamon sph or Nutmeg. Few
drops of lemon juice.

Method:

Wash and core apples, put int
baking dish & fill cavities (cream a b
with sugar & spice cover the bottom
the dish with boiling water. ~~dish~~
with boiling w) and bake in a
hot oven until soft. basting the
apples often with the sirup. Serve
hot with cream.

Coddled Apples.
Apple Sauce   Boiled Custard

65

Spiced Emergency Biscuit

2 c	8 T	flour
4 t	3/4 t	baking powder
1 t	spk	salt
2 T	1 t	shortening
3/4 c	8 T	milk or water
1 T	spk	cinnamon

Method: Mix and sift dry ingredients; cut in shortening with two knives and slowly add milk. Mix lightly. Drop carefully on pie tin. Bake in a hot oven from 10 to 15 min.

Dish Washing

1. Scrape dishes; all greasy dishes with a soft paper. Dishes with egg milk or dough adhering should be soaked in cold water.

2. Pile all dishes of one kind together.

3. Have plenty of hot water to rinse.

4. Wash glassware first silver second Chinaware third; Graniteware fourth knives, forks etc.

4. Lastly the tinware. Wash table rack and rds. Polish copper

5. Be sure all dishes are wiped thoroughly before putting away. Arrange

dishes neatly.

6. Wash and rinse dish cloth and towel
and hang up to dry.

Measurements.

3 t = 1 T
16 T (dry) = 1 c.
12 T (wet) = 1 c
2 c = 1 pt.
2 c = 1 lb.
4 c = 1 qt
2 pt = 1 qt
4 qt. = 1 gal.
8 qt = 1 bu.
4 pks = 1 bu
16 oz = 1 lb.
4 bu = 1 sack.

Milk and Water Bread.

1 c   4 T scalded milk.
1 c   2 T boiling water
1 T   1 t shortening
1½ t   ¼ t salt.
1   ¼ yeast cake.
1 t   ¼ t sugar.
¼ c   1 T lukewarm water
6 c   1 c sifted flour.

Method:
    Break yeast cake into sm

Cup Cakes.

⅔c – ½ T butter
2 c – 8 T sugar
4 – 1 T egg
3½ c – 5 T flour
4 T – ½ t baking powder.
¼ t – ~~mate~~ mace.
1 c – 1 T + 1 t milk.

Method: Cream butter & sugar.
Mix and sift dry ingredients.
Add beaten egg to the creamed
sugar; then add milk and flour
alternately. Butter pans careful.
Bake in a ~~hot~~ moderate oven
20 min. Cover with chocolate or
with boiled frosting.

Boiled Frosting.

1 c. sugar
⅓ c water
¼ t vanilla
1 egg white

Method: Stir sugar and water
until all sugar is dissolved.
Boil until a thread flys from
a fork. Beat white of egg.
Pour gradually over white of
egg and beat until spread over

Cranberry Pie

½ c cranberries
½ c water
¾ c sugar

Method:
　　　Make the sauce to fill the pie

Plain Paste.
1½ cup flour
¼ c lard
¼ c butter
¼ t salt
cold water? just enough to make a paste.

Method: Add the salt to the flour and
work in the shortening with the finger
tips or with two knives. Moisten the
flour with the water to make a dough.
toss on the flour board. knead into a
round ball, then roll in a thin crust.
Have the dough round in shape. Cut
off the outside, put in the filling. Cut
narrow strips. Lay across wise. Bake in
a moderate oven until nicely brown
along the edges and top.

Cristmas Cookies

2 T butter
¼ - ½ T sugar
1 egg
1 t baking Powder
¼ t salt
⅔ c flour + 2 T board
2 T milk

      Method:

Same as for peanut cookies.

      Frosting

1 c sugar
⅓ c cold water
1 egg white
½ t vanilla

      Method: Boil sugar and water
until syrup threads. Pour (until syrup
threads) carefully over egg white which
has been beaten stiff and dry. Beat
until thick enough to spread. Spread
with a knife over each cooky and let dry.

      Peanut Cookies.

2 T - 1 T butter	2 T - 1 T milk
¼ c 2 T sugar	⅓ c 5 peanuts
1 - 1 T egg	½ t - ¼ t lemon extract
1 t - ½ t baking powder	
¼ t spk salt	
⅔ c 4 T flour + 1 T for board.	

Method

Cream butter & sugar. Add milk & vanilla. Mix and sift dry ingredients. add to first mixture. Chop nuts very fine. Save ½ for to of cooky. Toss on a floured board and continue as for Vanilla Wafers. After all are cut, place the & nut pressing it in carefully on each cooky.

Chocolate Cake

½c 1T butter	1 ¾c - 6 T flour	
1c - 4T sugar	3 t - ¾ t baking P	
3 - 1T egg	1 t few drops of Vanilla	
½c 1T + 1T milk		

Frosting

1c sugar	⅓ c water
1sq chocolate	½ t vanilla

Method: Cream butter & sugar. Add beaten egg. Mix and sift dry ingredients. Add milk and flour. Last add vanilla. Boil sugar & water until the chocolate. To melt the chocolate. Cut chocolate fine and put in a cup and set in a place. (of)

Potatoes

Wash and peel very thin cut into small pieces add salt, boil into small clean water that as been salted, cook until ten.

Mash Potatoes

add a little more salt a springle of pepper a little milk and mash until flaky and smooth. For rice potatoes, put the whole potatoe (put the whole po) put th (whole potal) into the ricer and press.

Boston Baked Beans

Pick over 1 qt of beans, cover with cold wat and soak over night in the morning cover with fresh water, heat slowly and cook until it tender the skin burst drain bean, Add a piece of pork fat scrape the rind and cut it in pieces ½ in width put into bean pot and cover with beans mix a T of salt one T molasses and three T sugar a 1 cup of boiling water and pour over bean slowly. fix or 8 nine hours add and little water as it needed, then boil the beans add a little soda to soften the beans.

Rice Pudding with Raisins

½ c milk
c 1 T rice
¼ spk of salt
c 2 t sugar
c 1 T raisins
2 t lard.

Method. pick over the rice
wash. pour slowly into boiling
water cook until rice is tender
drain and wash into cold
water. put in baking dish and
add other ingredients bake in 2
min in oven.

1. Broiling, cooking over glowing fire   } direct
2. Roasting "   "   before "   .   application
3. baking " cooking in an oven   of heat.

                                         } application
                                         by means of
                                         heated oven.

4. Boiling " cooking in boiling water   } heated by
5. Stewing " cooking for long time in   means of
water below the boiling   water

6. Steaming: moist cooking a steamer   } by contact
dry : cooking a double boiler   with steam
                                         } by the heat
                                         of the steam
                                         surrounding
                                         the vessel.

7. Frying: cooking in hot ft deep enough to cover
the article
8. Sautering: cooking in a small quantity of fat

Serving

No 1. Have the room clea... well dusted and ai

No 2. Have the table in the center of the room directly in the gas fixture.

No 3. Lay on the silence cloth with ends and edges even silence cloth should be clean

No 4. Lay a clean wide table cloth which as been iron smothly with edges and corners over centers of the table.

No 5. Laying off the silence knife with sharp ends at the right spoons that are to be used except dessert spoons lay nept to knife & forkes that are to be used at the left.

No 6. Glass for water before the knife

No 7. Napkin clean white ironed smastly fold with a mongram up with the edges toward the right

No 8. Above the forks place the buttered knife across the butter plate.

No 9. A cover consist of plates glasses silver and napkin to be used by person The space occupy by 1 person with these things is 25 to 30 inches

No 10. Pass all food to the right left side except the water and coffee remove all dishes from the left except water and coffee Remove all large dishes from the tabl

first last lay the small one
Brush the crumbs with a napkin
folded over the hand into a plate. Then
serve the dessert never pile the dishes
one upon the other. Pass quickly & quietly
making as little noise as possible with
the dishes. Do not take silver from the
dishes. Cover the left hand with a
napkin.

Celery & Tomatoe Puree.

One bunch celery cut in one inch pieces
cook in 3 pints of water and salt to taste
cook until the celery is very soft. two T
of fat so pork fat.
One small onion sliced thin one carrot
sliced thinly. thin to small pieces of
parsely, two cloves, bay leave cook this
Tin min. Two cans of tomatoes, T of sugar
½ T of salt spk pepper 2 T of butter Two T
of butter cooked tomatoes, sugar salt &
pepper about 10 min. and pour through
the strainer rub carefully not to let it
lump. when thick add to the tomatoe
juice combine of three mixture and be
for a few minutes.

Butter Making.

a. If it rises to the top in form of globules. These are lighter then the other part of the milk rises as cream.

b. We beat or churn cream to make butter for cream butter we need clean cream and all dishes thourly clean.

c. After the butter is formed wash well to get out all of the milk. This milk contains casein which spoils quickly and if not washed out would spoil the butter.

d. add salt and mix thourly with the butter pake in a stone jar, or in a wooden tub. sweet butter contains no salt. sweet butter spoils quickly then salted butter.

e. fresh cream may be used for butter or sour cream is good. Cream & battle = 19 oz battle = 11.1 oz.

Cream weight 7.9 oz.

plate = 4.1 oz

~~Butter~~ Butter & plate 6.1 oz

Butter = 2 oz

2 oz C. 1/0 if 1 lb C. 80¢

Composition of Milk.

a. Milk + iodine gives a brown color. No starch.

b. Cream + iodine gives brown color. No starch.

c. Drop a little cream on unglazed paper. Paper looks greasy. There is fat in cream.

d. Use milk the same way. The paper looks greasy. There is fat in milk.

e. Pour 1 st of milk in a test tube. Air is in milk. Boil some milk. When little bubbles appear on the sides, the milk is scalded. When large bubbles break on the top the milk is boiling. Put a little scum is formed. Using a thermometer, we found on top of milk over scalded milk to be 184° (Fahrenheit) H. Using a thermometer to find the boiling point, the mercury went up 212° H. boiling point.

f. Put a little scum in a test tube and add ½ st vinegar. It became thick and looked like sour milk. This thick milk is called curd and the water part is called whey. To make sweet milk sour quickly, add some acid. Also let stand in a warm place if in no hurry. Curd rises to the top and the whey remains on the bottom. There is water in milk.

g. Milk has a sweet taste when fresh sugar
is in milk too.

H. human milk is called albumen. Did not
thicken very much when boiled last
when vinegar was added it became very thin
This albumen is called casein. Casein is a tissue
builder that is it builds up the body.

i. The milk thickens when we are added
vinegar. This thickening is coagulating.

j. Milk contains mineral matter. The mineral
matter helps to make bone. to keep our blood
pure etc.

K. sugar is an energy maker. Fat gives us fuel

Meat. Structure of Meat.

Beef has a deep red color. Egg white &
nitric acid + ammonia + heat give a yellow
color. This color shows that there is albumen
in egg. Beef + nitric acid + ammonia + heat
gives a yellow color. Therefore beef contains
albumen in meat is called myosin. The
albumen in blood is called fibrin. The
albumen in milk is called casein. The albumen in flour is called gluten. Heat sears
the out side of meat. Acid also sears White
is a thin skin like part found in between
the flesh. It is elastic. This is & the connective
tissue. Bundle consisting of many fiber like
hard squeeze reddish juice comes out. This
juice contains albumen which is fat called

Breaded Pork Chops.

Have chops cut very thin, sprinkle with salt and a slight bit of pepper. Place in a hot frying pan and sear on one side then turn and sear on the other and cook slowly until tender and well browned on each side. Roll cracker or bread crumb Beat up egg and add 1 T cold water to it dip the pork chops in the beaten egg then roll in cracker crumbs or bread put in the frying pan and brown on each side. Garnish with parsley and serve hot.

$$212° f. = Boiling Point$$
$$282° f. = for stewing.$$

Bone.

Examine ends of bone sawed in two.?
Where is the bone the softest, spongy, soft?
What is the meterial within the bone called?
Notice tough, fibrous covering on ends
Does bone break easy?
Burn a bone. How is it changed? Does it break early?
What part of the bone has been burned?
Composition of bone.

$\frac{1}{3}$ water

$\frac{2}{3}$ ($\frac{2}{3}$ m. m. + $\frac{1}{6}$ mineral Matter)

Mineral Matter = lime
animal " = fat & callagen & marrow
Cartilage Gristle.

		S. Price.
Neck - Stewing -		10 to 12¢
Chuck -	Pot roast or boiled stew	15 to 18¢
Ribs	Steak? Roast -	20 - 25¢
(loin)		20 - 25¢
Rump	Roast, corn beef, boiled	18 to 20¢
Flank	Flank Steak	16¢
Sut	boiled	8¢
Brisket	Pot roast, stew	12 to 15¢
Shanks	Soup	5 to 10¢
Round		16 to 28¢
2nd "		15 to 18¢

Nitric + ammonia + heat + bone juice → a yellow colo
it contains protein. This protein in bone is called
ossein, Kenand.

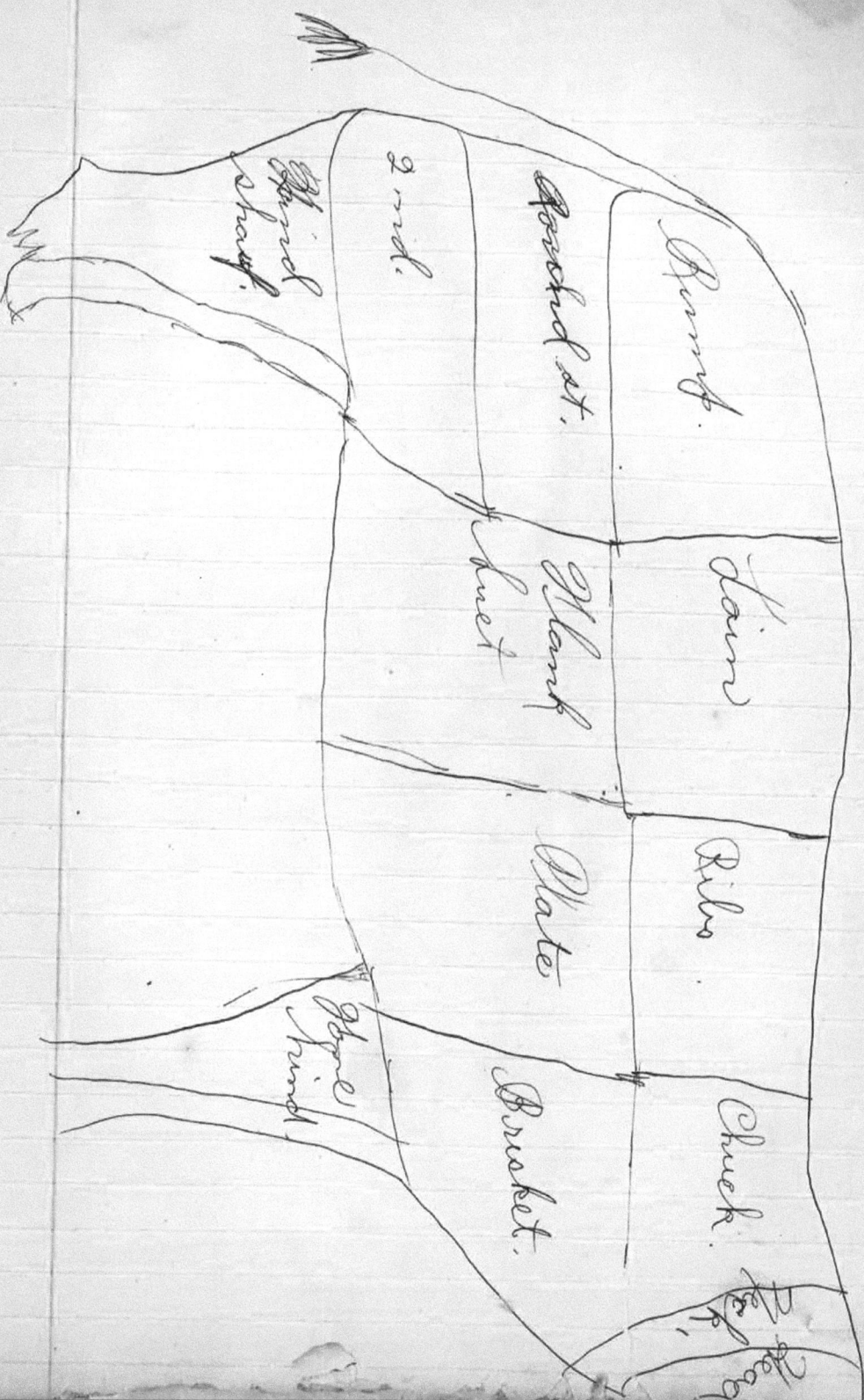

Rump.

Loin.

Round 1st.

2nd.

Flank

Suet

Ribs.

Chuck.

Flank
Shank

Plate

Brisket.

Shin
Shank

Pills.

Veal.

Veal is obtain from a young cafe. Kill when it is 6 to 8 weeks old. Veal contains less fat then beef pork or button mutton. It is less nutritious and more difficult to digest. Beef after killing should hang two or 3 weeks in winter and 2 weeks in summer. Veal ~~in winter~~ does not ~~surp~~ improve upon hangen, but should be eaten soon after killing and dressing, the flash of a young animals do not keep as long as old. Veal is divided in the same matter as ~~game~~ into the fore and hind quarters the fore quarter is divided into the brest shoulder and n The hind quarter into the loin, The leg and the knuckle. Cuttlets are sometimes cut from the leg

The good veal may be poen by its pink color and white fat. It has very little flavor and lacks ~~fat~~ cooking and more sneezing then other me

Cut veal   Veal Stew.

Cut veal in small pieces ~~add~~ and wash add salt onion and let simmer until tender. Have two teaspoo of flour in two T of water be carefull that their is no lumps when veal is cool add water and flour gradually. Stirring constantly.

The ends of the bone is the softest.
The outer side is the hard part
The inside of the ends is the sponse
The meterial within the bone is called marron
The tough fibrous part or covering on the ends

Cucumber Sweet Pickles

½ bu cucumbers. Cover with Alum
water 1 dessertspoon to 1 qt of water
Heat slowly until boiling point
then cool gradually. take from Alum
water and cover with cold ice water
if possible Make a syrup.
1 pt vinegar 2 lbs granulated sugar
2 tablespoon cloves & cinnamon tied
in a bag. Let syrup boil 13 min
remove cucumbers from cold water
to a crock and pour over the syrup.
Reheat syrup 3 or 4 mornings
successively ~~~~ and pour over
cucumbers.

Sour Pickles

Put pickles in a brine strong enough
to float an egg. Let stand 24 hrs.
Then put in cold ice water for
2 hr or let water run over them
for 2 hrs. Then crock and put
vinegar seal & put away.

Potatoes baked in half
shell.

Select 6 medium sized potatoes
and bake 30 min or until soft.
Remove from the fire cut in
half halves and scoop out the inside
carefully. Mash add 2 T butter 1 t salt
spk of pepper, and 3 T milk then add
the whites of 2 eggs and beat well.
Refill skins and bake again 5 to 8 min
in a very hot oven. Potatoes may
be sprinkled with grated cheese before
putting in oven.

Apple Pie.

3 C — 8 T flour
½ — 2 T Lard
1 t — spk salt
? — ? water.

Method:

Mix and sift dry ingredient
cut in shortening with two knives; add
jus enough water to make the dough
in two pieces roll one the size of the
tin line and press out the air. Wash
apples pare take off the core and slice
apple in tin slices, lay on crust sprinkle
with cinnamon and sugar. Roll out
second part. Cut a design in center so as to
let out the steam. Wet edges of the lower
crust. Lay on the top crust and press

Beverages.

Anything to drink.

Water is the most common Beverage

Water is essential of life.

All beverages contain a large % of water, and there uses are —

I. To quench the thirst.

II. To introduce water into the circulatory system.

III. To regulate body temperature.

IV. To assist in carrying off waste.

V. To nourish

VI. To stimulate the nervous system and various organs.

VII. For medical purposes.

Freshly boiled water should be used for making hot beverages.

Freshly drawn water for making cold beverages.

Liquors.

Rum

Whiskey

beer

wine

Brair Ridge

Gin

Her China Bishni

Beverages.

Water

milk

Cocoa

coffee

tea

Lemonade.

How to make tea.

1 t tea
1 c boiling water.
Method: Scald the teapot, put in
tea and pour on boiling water.
Let stand in a warm place 5 min,
strain it, serve immediatly with,
or without sugar and milk. Do not
steep the tea second time, Never oil
tea do not add leaves to those already
steeped.

Spiced Fruit Cake.

½ c ½ T butter   ¾ c - 2 T brown sugar.
¾ c - ½ T raisins   ¾ c - ½ T currants.
½ c - ½ T dates (chopped) ½ c - 1 T molasses.
2 - 1 T egg   2 c - 5 T flour.
½ t - ¼ t soda.   ½ t - ¼ t baking Powder
½ c - 1 T milk (sour) ¾ t - ¼ t cinnamon
½ t - spk cloves.   ½ t - spk mace.
½ t - drop lemon extract

Method. Cream butter and sugar; add the
molasses; mix well. Add the beaten egg.
Mix and sift dry ingredients thoroughly
Dredge fruit with flour. Add milk flour
and fruit alternatly. Add flavoring last
Pour into greased pan and bake in loaf for
in a (moderate) moderate oven about
1 hour cover with frosting.

Fish.

~~Codfish~~ Balls.

1 C fish
2 ~~ ~~ Potatoes.
1 egg
½ T shortening.
⅛ t . s/k pepper.
½ t - " salt.

Method: If codfish is used wash in
cold water and pick in every small pieces.
Cook fish in boiling water until tender.
When cooked drain and combine with the
ingredients. Wash, pare and cut potatoes in
small pieces. Boil until soft; drain and mash.
Add the beaten egg carefully to the potatoes.
Form in round balls plate cakes and fry in deep fat
until brown . (min allowed for browning,
a piece of dough. 40 sec for cooks.

Plain Cake.

⅞ c   ½ T butter   2 c   3 ct sugar.
4   1 T egg .   1 c   1 T & 1 t milk,
3½ c - 5 T flour   4 t   ½ c t baking powder
¼ t   1 ssp lemon extract.

Method: Cream butter & sugar add well beaten
egg. Mix well ingredients; add alternately with
milk to the first mixture. Add flavoring last.
Pour into a greased pan and bake in moder-
oven. Test with a toothpick or straw.
Loaf 45 to 60 min. Layer 15 to min.

Boiled Frosting.

1c - 3c sugar.
1/3c - water.

Put sugar in boiling water in a saucepan
and stir until sugar is dissolved. Beat gradually
until it boils. Boil without stirring, until
the sirup will thread, when dropped at the end
of the fork. add the beaten egg whites of the
egg and beat thick enough to spread, add
flavoring and spread on cake with a spoon
If not beaten long enough the frosting
will run. If beaten too much sugars it,
This frosting should be a glossy look.

Tea.

The dried leaves of a plant that
grows chiefly in China, Japan and India.
There are many kinds of tea but they
are all supposed to come from one kind of
plant, the difference being made by the
different soils and climate in which the
plants grow by the time of picking the
leaves and by the various ways in
which the leaves are cured.

The tea plant is a evergreen
shrub which when wild grows 4 to
5 ft high. (25 to 30) but which when
cultivated is kept pruned so that it is
usually a little less than a man.

Whole Wheat Bread.

2 c - 6 T white whole wheat flour,
1 c - 2 T white flour.
1¼ c - 3 T sour milk.
4⅓ c - ½ T molasses.
1/4 c 2 T sugar,
1 t ¼ t soda (¼ t baking powder,
1½ t ½ t salt,
1 - 1 T egg.
2 T - 1 T melted shortening.

Method:

Mix and sift dry ingredients, add
molasses to the milk add the melted
shortening then the beaten egg. Combine
mixture, place in a greased pan bake 3 ots
60 min.

Custard Pie.

½ of the amt of apple pie.

Custard Filling.

2 eggs 1 egg,
3 T salt sugar ½ t,
½ t salt. sp.
½ c. 5 T milk.
sp. sfk nutmeg.
½ t. 1/4 t,

Pie Plant birds nest.

2c	1/3 c flour	4 T	3/4 baking p.
1 T	- spk salt	1 T -	1 t shortening
3/4 c	- 3 T milk	3 T -	1 t sugar.

Use biscuit method.

? - 1/2 c rubarb or pieplant.

? - 1 t sugar.

? - 1/2 t cornstarch

Method. Mix sugar & cornstarch. Wash skin and cut rubarb into small pieces. Put into dish, sprinkle with sugar & cornstarch. Lay on dough and bake in a hot oven 15 to 20 min.

Rubarb Pie

Wash and skin rubarb and cut into small pie. lay on the pie mix the sugar & cornstarch sprinkle over the tops.   Paste

8 T flour

2 T shortening

spk salt

water to moisten

Baking Powder sponge Cake

1½ c sugar.

3 egg white

½ c boiling water.

2 t. baking powder.

1¾ c flour

¼ t salt

1 t. lemon extract or lemon juice

2 t. lemon juice.

Use the sponge cake method.

Popovers.

1

1 c – 4 T flour,

¼ t – o t salt.

⅞ c – 3 T 1 t milk.

1 – 2 t egg

1 t ¼ t shortening.

Method: Mix salt and flour add milk gradually in order to obtain a smooth batter add egg beaten well and melted shortening beat two min. turn into hissing hot buttered gem pans & bake 25 to 35 min in a hot oven. They may be baked in buttered earthen cups when the bottom with a glazed apperance Small round iron gem pans are the best. We found that the earthen cups are the best.

Pie Plant birds nest.

2c	1/3 c flour	4 t	3/4 baking p.
1 T	— spk salt	1 g —	1 t shortening
3/4 c	— 3 g milk	3 g —	1 t sugar.

Use biscuit method.

? — 1/2 c rhubarb or pieplant.

? — 1 t sugar.

? — 1/2 t cornstarch

Method. Mix sugar & cornstarch. Wash
skin and cut rhubarb into small pieces.
Put into dish, sprinkle with sugar &
cornstarch. Lay on dough and bake in
a hot oven 15 to 20 min.

Rhubarb Pie

Wash and skin rhubarb and cut into
small pie . lay on the pie mix the
sugar & cornstarch sprinkle over the
top.   Paste.

8 g flour

2 g shortening

spk salt

water to moisten

Grape Jelly.

? grapes.
? sugar
? water

Method: Stew and wash
grapes. Mash a few for mois-
ure. Cook carefully, when cooked pour into a jelly bag and
let drip. Measure juice Take
an equal amount of sugar,
Boil about 20 minutes or until
jelly jells. Drop on a cool plate
to test (Wrinkled appearance. Put
into sterilized glasses. Let cool,
Cover with parafin. Cover and
set away,

Chow Chow.

1 large cauliflower
1 qt green cucumbers.
3 doz small cucumbers.
2 doz   "   onions.
Soak cucumbers in brine for two
or three days. scould the rest in
strong salt and water. Add pepper
and whole cloves, allspice, and
stick cinnamon, as you choose.
Scald the following, stirring
constantly, and when well mixed

93

pour over your pickles: two
and a half quarts vinegar:
two and a half cups brown
sugar. one half cup flour: six
tablespoonfuls ground mustard
Bottle in sterilized jars. Seal.

Peaches.

4 Peaches.
1/3 c sugar.
Method Put sugar and water
together and stir constantly
over the fire until the sugar
is dissolved. When the sirup
boils skim it. Draw the kettle
back where the sirup will
keep hot but not boil, Wash
and pare peaches, cut halves.
remove core carefully. Put
fruit into preserving kettle
and cover with hot sirup.
When fruit begins to boil skim
carefully. Boil gently for 10 min
or if hard cook until it can be
pierced with a silver knife.
Sterilize jars, put in jars over
with sirup, wipe carefully, run
silver knife around insides carefully

Pears.

4 - pears.

1 - c. of sugar.

3/4 c - water

Method: Put sugar into water
and stir over the fire until
the sugar is dissolved. When the
sirup boils skim it. Draw the
kettle back were the sirup will
keep hot but not boil. Wash an pare
pears, cut in halves remove core
carefully. Put fruit into preserving
kettle and cover with hot sirup.
When fruit begins to ___, skim
carefully. Boil gently for 20 min;
or if hard cook until it can be
pierced with a silver fork. Steriliz
jars, put in jar cover with sirup,
wipe carefully, run with silver
knife around sides and seal fast.
Wash jars and set away for winter.

Plums.

12 - plums.

1 c - sugar

1/2 c - water

Method: Wash carefully. Drop
in boiling sirup. But do not
crush. Cook 5 min. Put in sterilyed
jars. Seal and wash jars and put
away.

Chile Sauce,

1 bu –	2 T tomatoes.
2 doz	4 onion
1 "	2 red pepper.
4 T –	¼ t cinnamon
2 T –	⅛ t claves.
4 T –	½ t celery seed.
2 qt –	2 T vinegar (cider)
4 lb –	1 T sugar.
2 c –	½ t salt,

Method :

Wash vegetable scald and peel tomatoes peel onion cut stem from peppers. Chop all vegetables very fine. Put in preserving kettle add other ingredients and boil steadily 1½ hrs. (small ½ hr.) Leave uncover for a short time and fill up those needing. Seal and set away in a cool dry place.

Get a new book and recopy this month's work

Cooking March 4, 1912,
Monday.

Cornmeal Muffins.

1 c	cornmeal.
3/4 c	flour.
1 t	salt.
2 t	baking Powder.
1/4 c	molasses or 1/4 c sugar.
3/4 c	milk
1 egg	well beaten.
1 T	melted butter.

Mix & sift thoroughly dry
ingredients. If molasses are
used add it to the milk. Add
milk gradually to dry ingredients and egg & butter. Bake
in a hot oven 25 min.

Breaded Fish.
Wash and string fish scale
if necessary. Salt slightly.
Fry in a very little fat a light
brown color. It may be dipped
in flour. In flour or cornmeal.
Break an egg & add a tablespoon
of water. Beat well. Have bread
of cracker crumbs rolled fine.
Dip in egg and then crumbs

with tomatoe Sauce. slice onions

Tomatoe Sauce.

½ can tomatoes, 1 t sugar, 1 small
bay leaf, ½ t salt, spk pepper.
4 t shortening, 4 t flour.

Method; Cook tomatoes, onions
to 20 with sugar, salt, pepper and
bay leaf. Squeeze and strain.
Rub through strainer. Melt
butter. Add flour gradually,
stirring constantly. Add hot
liquid. Stir carefully not to
let it lumpy.

Shamrocks.

Use same amount for baking
powder biscuits.

Salad.

Cream Carrots.

Wash & scrap carrots cut into
thin slices and dice shapes. Cook
in very little salted water until
tender. Serve with white sauce.

2 T butter, 3 T flour, 1 c milk, ½ t salt,
spk pepper. Melt butter until bubbles
add flour gradually, add
milk gradually, stirring well.

beat until smooth & glossy.

Stuffed Green Peppers.

Pineapple Jelly.

10 T — 2 ½ t gelatine C. Dr. Price's
1 c — ¼ cold water Trinity Dessert
1 c — ¼ grated pineapple.
⅔ c — sugar.

Method : Dissolve gelatine in cold
water. Add the pineapple and let
come to a boil stirring carefully.
Dip mold in cold water; fill and
set in a cold place to form.
Serve with cream and sugar.

Vegetable Bouillon.

2 T sugar
1 egg fat
1 pkg tomatoes
2 whole cloves
1 salt spoon pepper
1 onion (capsicum) ?
3 stalks celery or
1 qt celery salt
1 bay leaf
1 blade mace or ½ tt mace) grated
2 qts cold water
1 egg white

Method Put the sugar into
the kettle; let it brown and
stir until sugar is nicely
browned. Add celery and carrot.

cut very fine. Strew the cold
water. Add tomato and
seasonings. Bring to the
boiling point and skim. Let
simmer for 2 hrs and strain.
Add beaten egg white mix
throughly and bring to the
boiling point. Strain again
serve hot with crispes
bread sticks or crackers.
~ Look up Bouillon and
Consomme.

~~Stewed~~ Pea Salad.
Green

1 pt green peas can.
1 head of lettuce with boiled oil
dressing.
8 egg yolks, 3 yolks,
7 tsp Olive oil 1/4 c,
4 T vinegar
1½ T lemon juice
1½ t salt
8 t Powderdsugar
4 c whipped cream or sour milk (?)
~ Beat yolks slightly. Add dry
ingredients. Add oil very slowly
then vinegar, lemon juice. Cook
in a double boiler until thick a
cream or sour milk just before

...soning, a spk of red pepper
may be put to taste.

Frosting
Plain Frosting.
egg white
2 T cold water
3/4 c pulverized sugar.
1/2 t lemon juice.
few drops green vegetable
coloring.

Beat egg stiff & dry, add
water & sugar into egg. By at
thoroughly, then add flavoring
& green until a add coloring
Spread with a broad knife &
use more sugar if necessary,

Orange Marmalade
doz   sweet juicy oranges (sweet skins)
4   lemons,
3   sugar
3   water

Peel. yel Wash oranges & lemons.
Cut lemons in halves, squeeze out
the juice. Cut up one juicy
Cut oranges into thin tiny
thin pieces Cover with water
and let stand 24 hrs & the next
day boil until peeling is soft

Meat Pie.

Meat, Left over or
fresh.

2 c - 6 T flour
4 t - 2 t baking P.
1 t - spk salt
4 T - 2 t shortening
3/4 c - 2 T milk or water

Wash & salt meat.
Cook until tender
with salt, pepper
& little onion &
enough water
to keep from
burning (stew). Line baking
dish with dough crust, fill with
meat, cover with a top crust.
Bake 15 to 20 minutes in hot
oven.

Strawberry Short Cake

2 c - 2/3 c flour
4 T - 1 T shortening
4 t - 1½ t baking Powder
3/4 c - 6 T milk
1 t - ½ t salt
1 - ½ egg
¼ c - 2 T sugar

Method: Baking Powder
biscuit method.
Add egg to milk.
Pat and roll up two parts.
Spread first layer with butter.
Lay second. Bake in a quick
or hot oven 15 — 2 min.
Wash and hull strawberries

www.ingramcontent.com/pod-product-compliance
Lightning Source LLC
Chambersburg PA
CBHW061053090426
42742CB00002B/29